Tiffany and Company

Tiffany and Co Catalog

Paris, London, Geneva, Union Square New York

Tiffany and Company

Tiffany and Co Catalog

Paris, London, Geneva, Union Square New York

Inktank publishing, 2018

www.inktank-publishing.com

ISBN/EAN: 9783747798928

GIFTS.

THE question is so frequently asked, "What can you suggest for a present?" that Messrs. Tiffany & Co. have prepared the subjoined lists of some of the articles appropriate for such a purpose, to assist persons in making selections.

The constant addition of novelties, of course, renders any list in a measure incomplete; and in order that the facilities and extent of the different departments may be better understood, brief mention of each is herein made.

More particular descriptions will be furnished on request; or to persons known to the house or naming satisfactory references, a carefully selected assortment of articles will be sent for inspection on receiving advice as to the requirements and price.

JEWELRY.

ESSRS. TIFFANY & CO.'S stock of Jewelry, besides being the largest in this country, possesses many other attractions.

It exhibits the latest novelties of London and Paris, simultaneously with their appearance in the shops of those cities, and usually contains specimens from Denmark, Russia, Japan, India, Spain, and other countries less frequently drawn upon, besides the unique productions of their own workshops, which are not to be found elsewhere.

A complete assortment of goods of all the best American manufacturers may always be found in their cases, including a full line of medium-priced articles.

Persons wishing to have any idea symbolized in a piece of jewelry will do well to consult with Messrs. Tiffany & Co., as their designers are trained, and their shops organized, with reference to such special work.

SILVERWARE.

OR the current season Messrs. Tiffany & Co. have a larger and more comprehensive stock of sterling Silverware than they have ever before shown.

During the favorable conditions of the last summer, many new and attractive goods were made expressly for this season's retail trade, including silverware for household use, and artistic articles of peculiar interest.

As these goods were produced at the minimum cost, the prices are lower than similar goods have ever before been offered.

Tiffany & Co. will send on request estimates and designs for special articles, or advice to committees having charge of presentations.

They are also prepared to work special silver into articles of use or ornament, and persons wishing to have heirlooms, or silver from mines in which they are interested, wrought into forms, may be certain of receiving their own metal.

WATCHES.

HE Standard Tiffany Watches are constructed upon the latest scientific principles, combining simplicity, strength, durability, and time-keeping qualities.

The simplicity of construction renders them less liable to get out of order than more complicated watches, and reduces the cost to the minimum at which watches of the same grade can be produced.

Each watch is adjusted to temperature and position, stamped with the name of the house, and fully guaranteed.

Messrs. Tiffany & Co. have a full line of Ladies' Watches in plain gold, carved, enameled, inlaid, jeweled, and other cases, and complicated watches as follows :

Chronographs, marking fifth of a second.
Chronographs, with split second.

Watches, with split and independent fifth second.

Repeaters, striking hours and quarters.

Repeaters, striking hours and five minutes.

Repeaters, striking hours, quarters, and minutes.

Self-acting Repeaters, striking hours, quarters, and minutes.

Calendar Watches, showing day of month and week, and changes of the moon.

Messrs. Tiffany & Co. are agents in the United States for Messrs. Patek, Philippe & Co., of Geneva, Switzerland.

Frodsham and Jurgensen Watches.

DIAMONDS AND OTHER PRECIOUS STONES, AND DIAMOND AND GEM JEWELRY.

IN this department Messrs. Tiffany & Co. have long held the leading position in this country.

Their extensive connections abroad enable them to obtain the most correct knowledge of changes in the various markets, and their system of purchasing for cash secures the greatest advantages as to prices. Their stock is the largest to be seen in any one establishment, and comprises carefully selected Solitaire and Matched Diamonds, Pearls, Rubies, Sapphires, Emeralds, and all the jewels less generally known. The greatest care is exercised in the setting of their gems, and the designers and modelers engaged in connection with the jewelry workshops are qualified to produce novel designs for special objects, which shall not be seen elsewhere.

As all the diamond setting is done on their own premises, under the supervision of a member of the house, absolute security is insured for jewels intrusted to them for re-setting.

PLATED-WARE.

IFFANY & CO.'S Hard Metal Plated-ware is silver-soldered in every joint, and recognized as the most economical ware made.

Unlike the ordinary plated-ware, it possesses all the qualities of sterling silver, except intrinsic value, and is practically indestructible by family, hotel, club, or restaurant use.

It is in use at "The Baldwin," the new hotel in San Francisco, Delmonico's, the Union Club, the Brunswick, and many other public houses and private families. The articles are all made from special designs, possessing a distinctive style.

BRONZES.

ESSRS. TIFFANY & CO. devote their entire second floor to the display of a stock of Clocks, Mantel Sets and Artistic Bronzes, which includes all the best productions of art-workers in bronze, and is constantly increased by the accession of new pieces as soon as published.

This floor has more the appearance of an art museum than a salesroom; besides the gems of metal sculpture from France, Russia, Italy, and Germany, it contains a great variety of decorative articles of polished brass, which are made in their own shops. Examples of Cloisonné, Champlevé, Limoges, and other enamels, Repoussé copper and steel work, fac-similes of historical arms and armor, and other articles of vertu, combine to form the most interesting and varied collection ever offered for sale.

POTTERY AND GLASS.

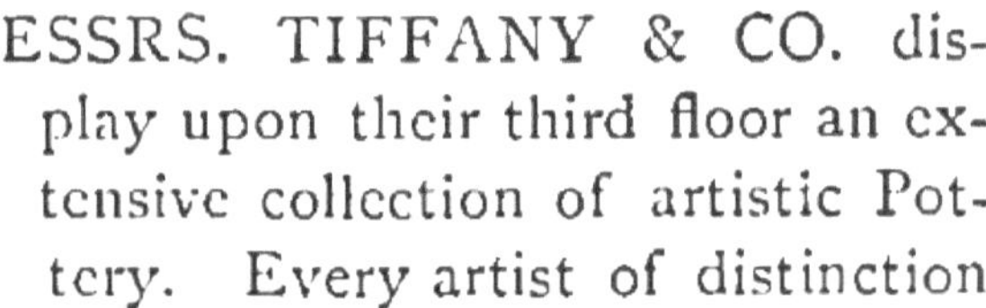

MESSRS. TIFFANY & CO. display upon their third floor an extensive collection of artistic Pottery. Every artist of distinction or merit, and every furnace of note is represented by choice selections.

In addition to the great variety of ornamental objects, they have a large stock of dinner, lunch, breakfast, dessert, and tea sets, from the lowest-priced decorated faience to the most costly porcelain, including the whole range of pottery.

Their stock of Glass-ware is most complete, and includes the plainest table-ware as well as the most elaborately engraved and cut.

STATIONERY.

TIFFANY & CO. furnish the correct styles of Wedding and other Stationery. They manufacture these goods on their own premises, and thus secure exclusiveness in style and the lowest possible cost.

Capable artists are prepared to execute heraldic devices, curious and original designs for monograms, ciphers, and other embossed headings, and skillful artisans to execute them in correct and beautiful colors.

Paper and Cards for Wedding Invitations are especially prepared from one pulp, securing a uniform texture and appearance in the various thicknesses requisite. Mourning paper and envelopes of new patterns in stock, or prepared with borders of any width to order.

Illuminated ménus and dinner cards of

unique designs are kept in stock, or special devices, expressing individual ideas, furnished on application.

Favors for the " German " and many other tasteful trifles are designed and finished in this department.

FANCY GOODS.

NDER this general head are included a variety of articles of use and ornament so great as to be almost innumerable.

Silver, gold, leather, wood, ivory, bronze, amber, tortoise-shell, and other materials are employed in their production.

Personal ornaments for ladies and gentlemen, convenient articles for the pocket, toilet, or library, and articles for yachtsmen, tourists, students, and others, are among the many.

In addition to the novelties from London, Paris, Vienna, and other European cities, Tiffany & Co. make in their several workshops goods for this department of a higher class than any of foreign manufacture, and specially suited to the expressed wants of their customers.

PRESENTS FOR LADIES.

(For lists of Silver Articles, see page 57.)

Bracelets. Bands, chain, and link bracelets.

Shopping Bracelet, with pencil attached, gold and silver, some richly jeweled.

Brooches.

Earrings.

Lace Pins.

Chemisette Studs.

Sleeve Buttons.

Cuff Pins.

Bangles.

MEMORANDA.

Shawl Pins.

Handkerchief Holders.

Fan Holders, worn as a chatelaine at the belt.

Sets of Brooch and Earrings. Cameos, coral, mosaic, enameled, onyx, amethyst, and a great variety of all gold sets, including all the novelties of the best makers of America, London, and Paris.

Lockets or Medallions. A great variety of original designs, including lockets appropriate for Bridesmaids, and for all occasions.

MEMORANDA.

Chatelaines, for bearing a watch, fan, vinaigrette, or other article.

Vinaigrettes.

Seal Rings.

Plain Gold Rings.

Chased "

Carved "

Enameled "

Rings, with small locket or other pendant.

Motto Rings, with various mottoes in French or English.

Cameo Rings.

Intaglio "

Fancy "

Cap Pins.

Hair Pins.

MEMORANDA.

Pencils.
Penholder and Pencil.
Seals.
Watch Keys.
Neck Chains.
Coral Beads.
Gold "
Onyx "
Mourning Jewelry. Almost all the articles of jewelry enumerated here may be had of onyx, jet, or gold, black enameled.
Bangles, with pendants and mottoes.
Brooches.
Earrings.

MEMORANDA.

Watch Chains. Opera chains are worn around the neck, and close with a slide, one end extending to the watch at belt. Guard chains pass around the neck, and extend double to the belt. Chatelaine chains are looped from belt to button-hole above, or to a brooch, and new chatelaines hang down from belt, with watch attached, and outside.

Lace Pins. A great variety, of novel designs.

Sleeve Buttons.

Combs, with ornamental backs of gold or silver, richly chased or engraved.

Lockets.

MEMORANDA.

Neck Chains.
Tea-cup and Saucer.
Silver-mounted Umbrellas.
Purses. Silver chain links with clasp, and long purses with sliding rings.
Glove Buttoners.
Shoe "
Shoe Horns.
Pocket Scissors.
Sets of Scissors in leather cases.
Tooth-Powder Boxes. Silver and ivory.
Ivory Boxes, to hold an ordinary bottle of extract.
Carriage Memorandum and Visiting Books, with cards and pencil.
Traveling Inkstand. Silver or leather.

MEMORANDA.

Glove Boxes.
Handkerchief Boxes.
Sewing "
Puff Boxes.
Odor Bottles. Silver or glass, richly cut.
Jewel Cases, self-packing; the soft cushions press on the jewels, no cotton or tissue-paper being needed.
Music Rolls.
Shoe Buttoners.
Glove "
Pomade Boxes.
Bonnet Brushes, for brushing velvet bonnets, etc.
Flower Holders, gilt and glass.
Pin Boxes.

MEMORANDA.

Bibles.

Prayer Books.

Hymnals.

Card Receivers. Gilt bronze, silver, bronze, polished brass, and pottery.

Paper Cutters. Silver, ivory, shell, and gilt.

Dressing Cases, with silver or silver-plated mountings.

Sets of Brushes.

Nail Boxes.

Shell Jewelry. Brooches, earrings, bracelets, bangles, lockets, watch chains, neck chains, crosses, sleeve buttons, chatelaines, full sets in cases.

MEMORANDA.

Puff Boxes.

Cologne Bottles. Silver or cut glass.

Hand Mirrors.

Bouquet Holders, for the hand.

Flower Vases.

Chatelaines, with one or more pendants, for fan, smelling-bottle, and other articles.

Bon-Bon Boxes.

Candlesticks.

Charity Bangles, with a small, round silver box attached to contain dimes.

Call Bells.

Card Cases.

Watch Stands.

Belt Clasps.

MEMORANDA.

Cloak Clasps.

Belts.

Vinaigrettes.

Odor Cases, of rare woods; some with richly gilt and enameled mountings.

Garters, with silver and gold clasps; some richly enameled and set with precious stones.

Shell Combs, with ornamental backs; some mounted with silver and gold. A great variety.

Ivory Combs.

Photograph Frames.

" Albums.

Traveling-Bags, with or without silver or silver-plated fittings.

MEMORANDA.

Shopping-Bags, of leather and velvet, with elaborate silver clasps, monograms and other ornaments.

Hand Mirrors, ivory or leather backs.

Glove Stretchers.

Sachets, silk and satin, painted with floral or other devices.

Fans. Lace, silk, feather, linen, and leather, with ivory, wood, mother-of-pearl, and tortoise-shell sticks. Special designs, expressing individual ideas, for bridal and other occasions, painted to order.

Opera Glasses. Leather, mother-of-pearl, ivory, enameled, gold, and richly jeweled cases.

MEMORANDA

Writing Desks.

" Cases, for traveling; containing all writing conveniences, including ink, folio, and an assortment of stationery.

Hair-Pin Boxes. Ivory and silver.

Decorated Candles. A great variety always in stock, and special designs painted to order, to harmonize with any style of candelabra.

Screen Mirrors. Silk covers decorated with flowers. The sides open, making an open square in which the side or back of head can be seen.

Laces. Lace covers for fans and parasols.

Silver Portrait-Frames, with secret for opening.

MEMORANDA.

Letter Scales, of gilt and enameled metals.

Perfumery, and Soaps. From Coudray, Société Hygienique, Lubin, Atkinson and Bayley, Johanne Maria Farina Cologne, and Patey's Brown Windsor Soap.

Aumonières. A velvet pouch to hang from belt, with silver clasps and monograms, and chatelaine to match.

Gaiter Hooks. Long, to button without stooping.

Tablets. To hang to chatelaine with ivory and silver covers.

Hair Ornaments of Silver. Arrows, daggers, pins with pendants, and other novel articles.

Court-Plaster Cases.

MEMORANDA.

Lace Parasols. Mounted with ivory, shell, coral, and gold.

Flower Holders. Glass, majolica and porcelain, from the principal furnaces of Europe.

Tête-à-tête Sets. Tea-pot, sugar-bowl, and creamer, with two cups and saucers, and tray.

Statuettes. Parian marble, Dresden China, and from all the leading furnaces.

Candlesticks. Majolica, Gien, Nancy, Wedgewood, and other wares.

Mirrors, with porcelain frames.

Coffee Cups. Sets of after-dinner coffee cups in cases.

Tea Sets. Decorated porcelain in great variety.

Berry Sets. Bowl, sugar-dish, and cream pitcher.

MEMORANDA.

PRESENTS FOR GENTLEMEN.

(For list of Silver Articles, see page 57.)

Vest Chains.

Guard "

Double Vest Chains, extending from the button-hole to both pockets, one end for watch and the other for pencil, safe key, night key, or other article.

Watch Keys and Seals.

Lockets of Gold or Stone. Suitable to be worn on watch chain.

Tooth Picks.

Gold-handled Knives, to hang from watch-chain, with steel blades and scissors.

MEMORANDA.

Pocket-Piece. Made from two double-eagles or two trade-dollars, hollowed out, and opened by touching a secret spring. They have a frame and glass for picture, and outwardly appear like a solid coin.

Gold Whistles.

Pencils, with gold pens.

Magic Pencils. Plain gold, and some studded with diamonds, pearls, turquoise, and other stones.

Sleeve Links.

Sets of Sleeve Buttons, Collar Button, and Studs.

MEMORANDA.

Sleeve Buttons. Gold, stone, mosaic, enameled, carved crystals, cameo, and set with precious jewels. Some, enameled to represent white linen, are much worn for evening dress.

Collar Buttons.

Cuff Buttons, to attach separate cuffs to wristbands.

Scarf Slides.

Scarf Pins.

Cameo Rings.

Intaglio Rings.

Charms. Innumerable tasteful devices, including compasses mounted in nautical and other styles.

Seal Rings.

MEMORANDA.

Gypsy Rings. In which a precious stone is buried in the heavy gold, leaving the surface only exposed.

Silver Jewelry; Tortoise Shell Jewelry. Comprising almost every article herein enumerated as of gold.

Serpent Rings. Plain gold and with jeweled heads.

Gold Suspender-Mountings.

Eye-glass Holders. To wear upon the breast of coat.

Water Pitchers.

Water Sets. Pitcher, goblets, and waiter, in cases.

Coffee Cup and Saucer.

MEMORANDA.

Soup Tureen. For individual use.
Butter Plate. " " "
Salt Cellar. " " "
Casters, with 3 bottles. For individual use.
Goblets.
Claret Pitchers, with silver lids.
Bells. For library or dinner-table, of silver, bronze, polished brass, and silver-plated.
Bell Trays.
Siphons. For decanting liquors.
Funnels. With strainers; points turning sideways, so the wine may run smoothly down the side of decanter.
Punch Bowls.

MEMORANDA.

Punch Ladles.
Toddy Kettles.
Nutmeg Graters.
Skewers. Five sizes.
Leg of Mutton or Ham Holders. With screw to secure it tightly.
Wine Labels.
Silver-mounted Corks.
Knife Rests. For supporting the carving-knife and fork when not in use.
Casters. With from two to six bottles.
Wine Stands. With two or three bottles.
Wine Coolers.
Ash Receivers.
Beer Mugs.

MEMORANDA.

Tankards.

Bottle Handle.

Sets of Carvers. With silver, ivory, mother-of-pearl, or buckhorn handles.

Silver Trowels. For use at ceremonious laying of corner-stones.

Spectacle Cases.

Napkin Holders. For keeping napkin up under chin.

Pocket Pincushions. Silver sides, suitable for engraving with name.

Razor and Shaving Brush, in case. With silver or ivory handles.

Whisks. With ivory handles, and blue or red silk loop and tassel to hang it by. Two sizes.

MEMORANDA.

Dog Collars.

Liquor Flasks. All silver; plain or richly ornamented.

Liquor Flasks. Glass, silver-mounted, some with two compartments.

Key Rings.

Soap Boxes. Plain silver, gilt silver, and silver-plated.

Shoe Horns. Silver, and ivory; some with shoe buttoner on the end.

Drinking Cups, that telescope and close compactly.

Boxes of Counters, with counters of mother-of-pearl.

Decanters, with silver mountings.

Coasters, for holding wine bottles.

Match Boxes. For the pocket; ivory, shell, wood, leather, silver, and gold.

MEMORANDA.

Match Stands. Silver, bronze, and leather; for house use.

Brushes. Hair, clothes, nail, tooth, and comb brushes, with wood, ivory, silver, shell, and lacquered handles, singly or complete sets in cases. Some with ivory handles of their own make, specially decorated in Japan.

Writing Cases. Containing a folio, inkstand, pens, and other fittings, and a supply of stationery.

Dressing Cases. With silver or silver-plated fittings.

Toilet Rolls. Compact leather rolls containing a few toilet necessities, very convenient to pack in a traveling-bag.

MEMORANDA.

Shaving Cups. Silver; some with strainer for soap, and others with attachment in which to burn alcohol to heat the water.

Portfolios.
Card Cases.
Russia leather, calf skin, snake skin, and morocco, with and without corners and edges of silver, or other metal.

Nail Boxes. Scissors, file, knife, scraper, nail polisher, etc., in leather, ivory, wood, and metal boxes.

Postage-stamp Boxes. Wood, leather, ivory, silver, and other metals.

Whist Counters.

Dominos. Ivory and mother-of-pearl, in attractive cases.

MEMORANDA.

Paper Cutters. Silver, ivory, tortoise-shell, lacquered and gilt, and enameled.

Bond Holders, with several pockets.

Segar Cutters. Mother-of-pearl or ivory handles, for the pocket.

Opera Glasses.
Field "
Marine "
Tourists' "
Tiffany & Co. are the sole agents in the United States for Messrs. Voigtländer & Sohn's celebrated glasses, which for scope of field, abundance of light, and brilliancy of the image, excel all others.

Liquor Sets. Glass tray, two bottles, and set of glasses.

Liquor Cases. Of rare woods, richly finished, with gilt mountings.

MEMORANDA.

Game Boxes. Containing chess, backgammon, and cribbage boards, dice and boxes, ivory counters, and playing cards.

Lap Tablets. For sketching or writing.

Mantel Sets.

Clocks.

Traveling Clocks.

Drinking Glass. In Russia leather or morocco cases.

Thermometers.

Barometers.

Pedometers. Carried in the pocket indicate upon a dial the distance walked.

Library Sets. Inkstand, candlesticks, pen, tray-bell, and other articles, of bronze and polished brass.

MEMORANDA.

Umbrellas. With gold, silver, ivory, and other mountings, and rare natural sticks.

A good silk umbrella is offered for five dollars.

Corkscrews. With silver, ivory, and buckhorn handles, for house use, and closing silver ones for the pocket.

Memorandum Books, with silver mountings.

Betting " " " "

Leather Purses, with silver clasps, for coin.

Pocket Books, with silver edges and fastening.

Suspender Buckles.

Fruit Knives, with and without nutpick.

Rules, 6 and 12 inches.

Penholders, handsomely ornamented, for the library.

Paper Knives.

MEMORANDA.

Check Cutters.

Tobacco Boxes, for the pocket.

" " for smoking tobacco.

Snuff "

Spurs.

Stirrups.

Horses' Bits.

Decanters. Cut, engraved, or plain glass, from the simplest to the most expensive.

Candlesticks. Bronze, silver, gilt, and polished brass, and silver, saucer-shaped to pack up.

Inkstands. Bronze, polished brass, marble, and glass, for the library, and leather, silver and other metals for traveling.

MEMORANDA.

Whistles. Silver and gold.

Coin Boxes. For holding gold coin or silver change.

Cigarette Cases. For the pocket, silver, leather with silver mountings, ivory, and tortoise-shell.

Segar Cases. Same styles as above.

Segar Lighters. Flint, steel, and combustible wick, with silver or gold mountings, for the pocket.

Segar Lighters, with alcohol lamps, for the dinner table.

Canes. Malacca and other woods, with ivory, tortoise-shell, silver, and gold handles.

Riding Whips.

Scissors. Some to fold up, for the pocket.

MEMORANDA.

Segar Boxes. Metal-lined boxes of rare woods, plain or richly mounted, to hold fifty, one, or two hundred segars, and with a compartment in the center for damp sponge to keep the segars from becoming too dry.

Traveling Bags, with and without toilet articles.

Smoking Sets. Including segar and tobacco holders, ash receiver, match stand, etc., of bronze and polished brass.

Telescopes, for yachtsmen.

Razors. Rodgers' and Lecoultre's, with silver, ivory, mother-of-pearl, and tortoise-shell handles.

MEMORANDA.

Papeteries. A convenient box containing an assortment of paper and envelopes.

They are made of rare woods, with richly gilt and enameled metal mountings, of leather, and of simple cardboard. Some of the latter as low as a dollar and a half each.

Gilt Goods. Inkstands, pen trays, library bells, candlesticks, segar and tobacco holders, traveling inkstands, paper folders, segar lighting lamps, letter scales, etc.

Jewel Cases. To drop in articles of daily use.

MEMORANDA.

Counters or Chips. Ivory, mother-of-pearl, and metal, in wood, leather, and metal boxes.

Riding Canes, with chamois loop for lash.

Writing Blotters. To place in library table or secretary.

Dress Coat Bags. For holding a coat without creasing, and a dress shirt without folding the bosom.

Calendars.

Traveling Candlesticks. For use in state-room of vessel, or to hang from lapel of coat, or from back of car seat in traveling. Closes compactly.

Majolica Inkstands.

MEMORANDA.

Smoking Sets. Beer Sets. " Mugs. Tankards. Beer Pitchers. Cracker Boxes. Cheese Dish and Cover. Tobacco Boxes. Broth Sets, on Trays.	Majolica, Doulton, and other wares from the principal furnaces of Europe.

PRESENTS FOR INFANTS.

Silver Mugs.
" Cups and Saucers.
" Bowls.
" Porringers.

MEMORANDA.

Silver Pap Boats.
" Plates.
" Knife and Fork, in case.
" Knife, Fork, and Spoon, in case.
" Fork, Spoon, and Napkin Ring, in case.
" Sets, including all or any part of the above, put up in handsome cases.
" Rattles.
Coral and Silver Bells.
Biting Pieces. Mother-of-pearl, silver mounted.
Strings of Amber Beads.
Armlets. Gold and coral.
Coral Beads.
Handkerchief Pins.
Sash Pins.
Feeding Spoons.

MEMORANDA.

Feeding Trays.
Finger Rings.
Ivory Cup and Ball.
Safety Pins, of gold and silver.
Toilet Sets. Ivory-handled brushes, with puff box, comb, and rattle in case.

PRESENTS FOR HOUSEKEEPERS.

Clocks, of marble, Mexican onyx, bronze, ormolu, polished brass, faience, cloisonné enamel and carved woods. Appropriate for library, dining-room, bed-room, sitting-room, boudoir, parlor, or hall.

MEMORANDA.

Traveling Clocks, with alarm, and that repeat at will and strike.

Night Clocks, with dial to illuminate with taper.

Limoges Enamels. Pitchers, vases, plaques, cups, card receivers, goblets, candlesticks, jewel and glove boxes. Some being reproductions of the works of earlier periods.

Cloisonné Enamels. Clock sets, vases, card receivers, segar-stands, candlesticks, inkstands, matchstands, pen trays, bells, candelabra, glove boxes and jewel boxes.

MEMORANDA.

Polished Brass clocks, candelabra, vases, candlesticks, inkstands, card receivers, pen trays, match boxes, jewel boxes, ash receivers, library sets, bells, etc.,

Bronze Statuettes. Large pieces for pedestals, and smaller ones for cabinets, mantels, clocks, etc., including a great variety of subjects both from the antique and the works of modern artists.

Bronze Animals. Small and large, by Mêne, Clessinger, Carnari, Bonheur, Dubucand, Parmantier, Fremiet, Barye, and others.

MEMORANDA.

Bronze Busts of different sizes. Poets, statesmen, philosophers, and other eminent persons, appropriate as presents for professional men.

Vases.
Card Receivers.
Candelabra.
Candlesticks.
Inkstands.
Bells.

Of bronze, polished, brass, oxydized silvered bronze, Limoges enamel, cloisonné enamel, ormolu, nickel, onyx, marble, etc.

Pen Trays.
Ash Receivers.
Match Stands.
Paper Weights.
Jardinières.

MEMORANDA.

Andirons. Polished brass.

Fenders.

Tongs and Shovel. Polished brass and iron.

Coal Scuttles. Brass.

Thermometers. Obelisks, Column Vendome, and other forms.

Hanging Lamps. For burning a taper at night.

Library Candlesticks. For one or two candles, with shades.

Moderator Lamps. Polished brass, faience with gilt mountings, decorated porcelain, cloisonné enamel, etc.

Sconces. Polished brass, bronze, silvered and oxydized, with mirrors, metal or decorated tile centers, and for 2, 3, 4 or 5 candles.

MEMORANDA.

Brackets. Polished brass, and wood with brass mountings.

Pedestals. Marble, bronze, Mexican onyx, ebony and other woods.

Dinner, Dessert, Tea, Luncheon, and Breakfast services, of every grade, from the simplest faience, to the most elaborately decorated porcelain, including the whole range of pottery.

Center Pieces.

Compotiers.

Dessert Plates.

Oyster Plates.

Fish Services. In the form of shells.

Jelly Plates.

MEMORANDA.

Coffee Cups. Small cups for black coffee.

Plaques. For hanging upon the wall or standing on sideboards or cabinets. Decorated by eminent artists.

Jardinières. From the principal furnaces of Europe.

Garden Seats.

Vases.

Statuettes.

Umbrella Stands.

Pedestals.

MEMORANDA.

TABLE GLASS.

Compotiers.
Berry Dishes.
Center Pieces.
Goblets.
Finger Bowls.
Claret Decanters.
Sherry "
Liquor Bottles.
Water "
Pitchers.
Ice-Cream Dishes. For bricks or other forms of ice-cream.

Glasses for
Claret,

MEMORANDA.

Sherry,
Hock,
Champagne,
Liquor,
Ice-Cream, and
Punch.

SILVER ARTICLES FOR WEDDING AND OTHER PRESENTS.

From $10 to $50.

Olive Spoons, in case.
Cream Ladles, " "
Sugar Lifters, " "
Pickle Knife and Fork, in case.
2 Sugar Spoons, " "

MEMORANDA.

Sugar Sifter and Cream Ladle, in case.
1 Preserve Spoon, " "
2 " " " "
Berry Spoon, " "
" " and Sifter, " "
Ice-Cream Knife, " "
Pudding Knife, " "
Pie Knife, engraved, in case.
Crumb Knife, " " "
1 Doz. Coffee Spoons, gilt, in case.
1 Doz. Egg " " " "
1 Doz. Ice-Cream Spoons, in case.
1 Doz. Nut Picks, " "
Soup Ladle, " "
Oyster Ladle, " "
Punch Ladle, " "

MEMORANDA.

Salad Tongs, in case.
Salad Spoon and Fork, in case.
Fish Knife and Fork, engraved, in case.
Soup and 2 Gravy, in case.
Oyster and 2 Gravy, in case,
Asparagus Tongs, " "
1 Doz. Table Spoons, in case.
1 Doz. Tea Spoons, " "
Pair of Vases.
Pair of Salt Cellars and Spoons, in case.
Pair of Peppers, " "
Pair of Napkin Rings, " "
Mustard Pot, " "
Bell and Bell Plate, " "
Ash Receiver, " "

MEMORANDA.

From $50 to $100.

Ice-Cream Sets, gilt, in case, 13 ps.
" " " " " " 15 "
Ladle Sets, gilt, in case.
Punch Ladles, gilt, in case.
Mustard and 2 Peppers, gilt, in case.
Sugar Bowl and Cream Pitcher, gilt, in case.
Card Receivers, "
Segar Holders, "
Flower Vases.
Engraved Waiters, 8 to 12 inches,
Sugar Vases.
Creamers.
Hot Milks.
Butter Dishes.

MEMORANDA.

Olive or Pickle Set.
Small Fruit Dishes.
Pocket Flasks.
Toast Racks.
Celery Vases.
Tea Caddies.
Pair Goblets.
Pitchers.
2 Salt Cellars and Spoons, in case.
Sardine Boxes.
Porringers.

From $100 to $200.

Fruit Bowls.
Nut Bowls.
Ice-Cream Bowls.

MEMORANDA.

Ice Bowls.
Center Pieces.
Card Receivers.
Casters.
2 Gravy Boats.
Sugar Dessert Dishes.
Pitchers.
Tête-a-tête Sets.
Cake Baskets.
Segar Stands.
Butter Dishes.
Waiters, Oval and Round, 12 to 16 inches.
Pickle Stands.
Salad Dishes.
Sugars and Creams.
Chocolate Pitchers.

MEMORANDA.

Pair Goblets.
Egg Boilers.
Tankards.
Toddy Kettles.
Oyster Tureens.

From $200 and Upward.

Fruit Bowls.
Center Pieces.
Punch Bowls.
Wine Stands.
Tea Kettles.
Coffee Urns.
Wine Coolers.
Large Waiters.
Pitchers.

MEMORANDA.

Soup Tureens.
Vegetable Dishes.
Sets of Meat Dishes.
Fish Dishes.
Tea Sets.

MEMORANDA.

VERY article in MESSRS. TIFFANY & CO.'S establishment has the price in plain figures attached, from which no reduction is ever made.

Hence, persons at a distance from New York, ordering goods by letter or telegraph, may be certain that they pay no more than if the purchases were made in person, and they also secure the services of persons of experience and judgment in making selections. All articles sent in response to such orders, may be returned if not altogether satisfactory, and, if they have been paid for, the money will be returned.

Zeitfracht Medien GmbH
Ferdinand-Jühlke-Straße 7
99095 Erfurt, Deutschland
produktsicherheit@kolibri360.de